Honeycomb For Young Cubs, Vol. 1

Honeycomb For Young Cubs, Vol. 1

The nature of Father bears to Cubs:

"Male grizzly bears are often absent fathers who leave the female to raise the cubs. They are also known to kill and eat cubs, including their own, to regulate the bear population or to mate with the mother. Male bears are considered absentee fathers who do not help raise the cubs. They may even kill cubs that aren't their own."

Fathers, dads, uncles, brothers – this is where we end that generational curse. Now is the time for us to be at our best.

Honeycomb For Young Cubs, Vol. 1

Alpha.

Honeycomb For Young Cubs, Vol. 1

We grow too soon old, and too late smart.

Risk reward. Always know if the risk justifies the reward.

Ignorance is not the same as innocence.

You can't live twice. You gotta go now.

If you live the life that you love, then you'll love the life that you live.

You lay in shit too long, you stop smelling it.

The greatest threat to this world is a prayerful man or woman.

Ignorance usually never stops with a warning.

Watch how you come or watch how it go.

No one should die without trying.

Just because you boo LeBron doesn't mean you're going to stop him from scoring.

Cool things ain't cheap and cheap things ain't cool.

The grind won't come to you, you got to go get it.

Life is a balance of holding on and letting go.

Honesty is not synonymous with truth.

The answer to all questions is money. All answer for how to get to Heaven is God.

Attitude dictates altitude.

Bravery is not the absence of fear; bravery is overcoming fear.

Arrogance and self-awareness rarely goes hand in hand.

Good fences make good neighbors.

Your voice is your power. Education is the engine. Wisdom is fuel.

The only debt we owe our friends is loyalty and trust.

Learn to put yourself first and understand your self-worth. Know your own worth, you then understand others' value.

Shoot, shovel, or shut the fuck up.

Honeycomb For Young Cubs, Vol. 1

To look clean in front of thousands means you got to be willing to make it rain sweat and lay it all out in front of nobody.

We are all flying to either Heaven or hell, make sure you're packed.

Being without God is like a cowboy with no horse to ride.

You're born either an oak or a willow. You can't teach toughness.

If you have bad brakes on your temper, then you will hit someone or crash.

We are all born male and female, but we must learn to become men and women. We learn "protect, provide, and praise our family' from our father. We learn 'life, love, and tough lessons' from our mom.

Parley your passion into profit.

How do you think you live like me? Rhetorical.

Discretion is the better part of valor.

The dead don't cause problems. It's the living that you have to worry about.

If you don't know what you want to be, then at least know what's important to you.

Ignorance is not the same as innocent.

Rather be dead wrong than dead and gone.

Always have a plan, and two more backup plans to your backup plan. Not having a plan leads to helplessness. Helplessness leads to hopelessness.

Good luck for one man is always his brother's misfortune.

Two truths cannot occupy the same space.

The highest human act is to inspire.

Know thyself.

You can't dream of a face you've never seen. Don't be afraid to dream of yourself as a success. Someday it will become true.

Work hard. Stack cake. Play later. Rest. Repeat.

No risk it, no biscuit.

Honeycomb For Young Cubs, Vol. 1

Choose a career that will make you proud, and one that you enjoy getting up to go perform at your best...At your highest level.

Defeat is momentary. Success is monetary.

Yesterday, you said tomorrow.

The only way to know where the line is, is to cross it.

You can't afford anything that you can't buy five of something.

A bad dress rehearsal leads to a great opening night.

The choices we make are reflections of, and ultimately future manifestations, our character.

Try to laugh without smiling. It is impossible to contain happiness.

You were all I had. And now, I have me.

I never only want to give you things to make up for lost time. I wanted the time and space to instill in you, pour into you, raze you.

Mercy is from a position of strength. Vulnerability is from a position of unpreparedness.

Only the guy not rowing has time to rock the boat.

A man is lucky who knows what he wants to be in life. That man will never work a day in his life.

Nothing haunts more than things left unsaid.

The hardest choices require the strongest will.

Purpose makes a man, or woman.

Never wake up to be mediocre. Be great daily.

Every strong man should partner with a strong woman, and vice versa. Otherwise, someone will be emotionally carrying the other.

A woman is like a tea bag; you see how strong she really is once she's in hot water

Never lose the joy that you had as a child, always remember to be joyful.

When things go down, you go hard.

When you get back up, you go off. When you do get up, get even.

Honeycomb For Young Cubs, Vol. 1

When people leave you, they take a part of you with them. Don't worry about replacing them, you can always replenish what was taken.

Family and money don't mix. Never loan family money. If you can afford to give them what won't hurt you or your budget, then just give it to them.

If you loan money and they repay you, then count that a blessing. Fake friends never repay their loans. Never be that fake friend. If a friend borrows money and never repays you, then whatever that amount was that went unpaid count that as the cost of learning their true character. Never count that as a loss; always count that as a lesson.

When a toxic person attempts to control you, they will try to control how others see you. The misinformation will feel unfair but stay above it...trust that other people will eventually see the truth.

What is lost can never be saved.

If when you look at the people in your circle and do not get inspired, then you don't have a circle. You have a cage.

There is no such thing as being on time. You're either early or you're late.

The only fair thing in life is death.

Manage never panic.

For your leisure, one should strive to do the things that make you lose track of time.

I ONLY salute you if you're a boss. I ONLY shake your hand if I respect you. But I will have a conversation with anyone.

You lost me when you crossed me.

Happy endings are just stories that haven't finished yet.

Emotional toughness. Have that.

You ain't gotta lie to ride, ain't gotta pretend to win.

Remember to ice the swelling.

Choice is the consequence of your situation.

There's no full-time benefit for doing anything part time.

When you are an underdog in anything, you have to take what's yours. Nothing is given.

Honeycomb For Young Cubs, Vol. 1

It's a difference between a risk and a gamble. If you don't know the difference, there's your answer.

Anybody can do it, but you get rich if you do it well.

Be true to it not new to it.

Grind, get money, repeat.

A man should look as if he had bought his clothes with intelligence, put them on with care, and then forgotten all about them.

Celebrate the highs. Respect the lows.

Karma isn't a bitch, she's a mirror.

You can't catch your blessings if you're still holding grudges.

Hard things come before good things.

You can't compete when you can't compare.

The future won't make itself.

No amount of money ever bought a second of time.

Sometimes, it's business. Sometimes, it's personal.

Two types of people get shot, criminals and victims.

Pressure bust pipes.

There are good and bad ships, but the best ships are friendships.

In this world, you're either somebody or nobody.

We never lose our demons; we only learn to live above them.

When you befriend and make pets out of the monkeys on your back, you got to feed them.

Service to others is the rent you pay in order to enter heaven.

Dealing with someone that lies all the time ain't worth the 1:59.

Honeycomb For Young Cubs, Vol. 1

No matter your condition, maintain your mindset.

There's no such thing as love at first sight if love is blind.

Only a good man can start with little and gain much. More often, it is a bad man that starts with much and ends up with little.

You are judged by the company you keep by people who watch you from a distance.

Loyalty is far greater than any act you can do for someone.

Avoid people that act dirtier than Flint water.

What's more important, the flower or the soil?

I speak from the heart, so I rarely talk a lot.

You never realize how far away you are from your goals until you're standing directly in front of them.

I speak from the heart, that's why I don't talk much.

Starve your distractions. Feed your focus.

Patience allows the underdog to get the upper hand.

Money talks, bullshit walk...a mile a minute.

If it ain't beneficial it's artificial.

Almost healed means that you're still hurt.

Don't get bitter. Get better.

There is no such thing as wins and losses. Only wins and lessons.

Dreams do not make you successful. Hard work, sacrifice, and a little luck does.

Good luck for one man is always his brother's misfortune.

When you play silly games, you get silly prizes.

In for a penny, in for a pound.

Honeycomb For Young Cubs, Vol. 1

Never judge a man on where or what he drinks, but how he holds his liquor.

It's not how good you've been doing; it's how long you've been doing good.

Love is pain. Pain is paid in grief. Grief transcends value. Grief is worthless.

Dying is easy. Living is hard.

If you don't bump into the devil three times a day, then you are walking with him.

The bold may not live forever, but the cautious do not live at all.

Say less. Get the most.

Transform failure into fuel.

Work through adversity.

When you look in the mirror and feel defeated, it feels like two against one.

We grow through what we go through.

Difficult choices require strong will.

I don't care what people say about me, as long as it's not true.

Always maintain the courage of your convictions.

There are three tenets of life that must have reciprocity: love, loyalty, and respect.

And after you have suffered a little while, the God of all grace, who has called you to His eternal glory in Christ, will himself make you firm, strong, and steadfast. 1 Peter 5:10.

Love is bleeding through the night, scabbing during the day. Don't pick at it; let it do what it do and allow it to heal. The more intricate the scars, the truer the love.

You don't know who you are until you fail.

If you struggle to plan, make plans to struggle.

Practice makes perfect. Perfection makes paper.

Reputation is what people think of you. Character is who you are.

Honeycomb For Young Cubs, Vol. 1

Hope is a dangerous thing, for the faithless.

You don't know someone until you know what they want.

A smart person can play dumb, but a dumb person can't ever play smart.

We all have similar dreams but different mistakes.

How do you spell love? t-i-m-e

Friendship means little when it's convenient.

Fools talk. Cowards are silent. Wise men listen.

A man's ambition should not exceed his worth.

How a man does something is how he does everything.

If you don't make time for your wellness, then you will be forced to make time for your illness.

Attraction + obstacles = desire

Vision. Plan. Execution.

I'd rather shit in my hand and clap before I cross my own brother.

Life is not about the number of breaths we take, but about the moments that take our breath away.

Bad relationships are for people just waiting for something better to come along.

You cannot catch blessings if you're holding grudges.

Feed your focus. Starve your distractions.

Sometimes you have to keep your head down to see what's up.

Reputation costs a lifetime.

Successful people make the difficult look easy. People who fail make the easy look difficult.

Honeycomb For Young Cubs, Vol. 1

None of us deserve it, but we push forward anyway.

If you never ask, the answer is always no.

I'm around you if I can learn from you or got a genuine concern for you.

Heavy is the head that wears the crown.

Idle hands do the devil's work.

Life experiences come from the choices we make.

Destiny is a hard thing to run from.

Wake up and get your cake up. Your destiny ain't gonna come to you.

Haters comb through your life hoping to pick you apart.

With patience, and with an ability to suffer delayed gratification, a person can go from drought to drenched.

From broke to bespoke, that's me.

Man serves three masters on Earth: love, pain, and fear.

The punishment of a liar isn't that no one believes their lies, but their inability to believe anything from anyone.

One day, one win.

You can't clean a floor with a bucket of dirty water.

In life, you get what you work for not what you wish for.

No handouts.

Don't do something that only last 25 seconds but can get you 25 years. Think smart.

Life is hard. Life is even harder when you're stupid.

Hope is an emotion. Optimism is a mindset. Success is action.

Selfish people somehow want the most but always give the least.

Honeycomb For Young Cubs, Vol. 1

Anybody willing to put in hard work will always have dirt under their fingernails.

You have to give all of yourself to something if you are ever to reach greatness.

Skill requires repetition.

If you dominate for a year, it's your season. If you dominate a few years, it's your era. If you dominate a few decades, it's your dynasty.

If you have $10, spend only $3 and save $7. This is how you achieve wealth and stay prepared for a rainy day.

Change and blessings come only with time.

Correlation does not equate to causality.

Two wrongs do not make a right. Two Wrights did make an airplane.

Having a plan and doing it are two different things.

Be the best you. Be yourself. Don't ever try to be like another man.

Find happiness in all your choices, all that you do. There will certainly be obstacles and setbacks, however this is part of life. What matters is how you accept and overcome them. This is what measures your character.

When it comes to your individual mental peace and stability, refuse to be anything but okay. Guard your peace.

When in a relationship, you will learn ugly lessons from a pretty woman/handsome man.

A person's politics is just like their religion: it doesn't require you to believe the same, nor does it require your opinion.

Freedom is an illusion. No man's actions are free from consequence.

Have you ever seen a chrome crown?

Removed listening is insulting, people feel that you're not engaged or involved. Reactive listening is infuriating, you're taking everything personally. Responsible listening is listening as usual. Receptive listening is empathic; it tries to genuinely understand and respond to the other person.

Honeycomb For Young Cubs, Vol. 1

Unprecedented doesn't have to mean defeated. Allow the unknown to be opportunity for innovation.

Love + Honor + Loyalty = Family.

Opportunity is on the other side of chaos.

Everybody's mad at you when you are living fabulous, self-made mean never out here kissing asses.

New levels bring new devils.

Money is like water. If you pitch your tent, make sure it's near a source that can easily be accessed and can be replenished. Make sure it's a clean source, not dirty. Don't walk around this world looking and being thirsty - not a good way to be, not a good look. Make sure you're not caught in a drought and unable to sustain yourself. You can die of dehydration, so keep plenty of 'water' nearby.

The price of greatness is responsibility. Responsibility is an investment.

You can't make the same mistake twice, the second time it's no longer a mistake, it's a choice.

Knowing who you are is hard. Eliminating who you are not even harder.

In this world, a man just wants to be treated like a king in his own home. At home, we just want our partner to love us without condition. Nothing more.

I'm so ahead of my time, I'm about to start another life.

Respect is not earned twice, once you lose it then it's gone.

Better to be seen than viewed.

Grind all winter, shine all summer.

Paranoid of poverty.

My drive...25/8 no brakes.

Resistance to tyranny is obedience to God.

Nine out of ten worries are usually unfounded and self-imposed.

Honeycomb For Young Cubs, Vol. 1

We work with what we have, not what we wish for.

Getting out of something is always tougher than getting in.

Paradise lost is paradise gained.

People don't know your whole story; they just know the chapter they met you on.

Many are called yest few are chosen.

Rise and grind. Wake up and cake up. Don't sleep your life away.

Do the best with what God gives you.

When you're fighting with yourself, against those demons and monkeys on your back, and you're losing that fight.... what comes next is you fighting those closest to you. Taking an unnecessary fight to them that they did not deserve. Don't do that.

Never plan for a setback. Always plan for a comeback.

Put your tongue in park. Never run your mouth.

Do not be a fake like a fire drill.

A smooth sea never made a skilled sailor.

Isn't it fun to try to do the impossible?

You like someone for their qualities but love them for their defects.

If they did not invite you, don't ever ask to go.

What makes a man a man? Is it his origins? His views on life? I don't think so. It's the choices he makes. Not how he starts things, but how he decides to end them.

Wisdom is peace. Ignorance is chaos.

You will never win at life if you lose your mind.

Because you are alive, everything is possible.

Time is wealth, share it generously with family and friends.

Act your wage.

Honeycomb For Young Cubs, Vol. 1

Don't hate on anybody and don't wait on anybody.

If something is to be empty, let it be your stomach but never your pockets.

What you would do eventually, you should do immediately.

Trouble never sends a warning.

Life is what your soul costs. Make life worth it.

Don't strive to make news, strive to be the main topic.

Admiration can easily turn into hatred, which then also turn into suicide of self.

Have a funeral for all your bad habits.

I don't trust a man that puts his back against the wall. I trust a man that puts his back against the cross.

We're all links in a chain.

FEAR - false evidence appearing real.

Where you stand is where you sit.

When it comes to family, we can either hang together or hang separately.

If you don't talk about it, you're not working on it.

Rise and grind.

You can't break a stick that's part of a bundle.

Belief isn't what you say, it's what you do.

When you're a lion, you have to walk slow and growl low when around sheep.

If people are tired of how you live, they will die exhausted.

Stop at nothing if you're after something.

Subtract everything out of your life that's not adding up.

Honeycomb For Young Cubs, Vol. 1

Make shit shake until it break.

Every day is a payday, no days off.

When you make cake and get bread, you accumulate calories.

The future is now.

Living ain't for everybody, most people are waiting to die.

Avoid trick knowledge.

Love is the highest elevation of understanding.

Time is the currency of progress.

Straighten up or get your ass tore up.

Success is not a straight line.

There is no heaven without dying.

Toast - May we always get what we want, but never what we deserve.

Toast - Good bread, good meat. Good God let's eat.

Make your mess your message.

Good seeds make good trees.

Never mix your feelings with your dealings.

Being blind is having sight but no vision.

What can't be cured must be endured.

In life, there are no instant rebates.

Do not ever let anyone get the best of you, even if they want the best for you.

You can always make something out of what you've been made out to be.

We accept the love that we think we deserve.

Honeycomb For Young Cubs, Vol. 1

In life, no one wins...one side just loses slowly.

I have two words for you: two words.

Sometimes when you elevate, friends separate.

Man's reach exceeds his grasp. Man's grasp exceeds his nerve. Man's nerve exceeds his imagination.

Reach beyond your own bubble.

Come from ordinary beginnings, then achieve extraordinary accomplishments.

Existential dilemmas....do or don't. Will or won't.

Drink the stress, gargle the pain, and spit bullshit out of your system.

Save until it hurts.

Pigs get fat, hogs get slaughtered.

Give way.

Be where your feet are.

Hope not, hope gets the poorly prepared killed.

I'm an acquired taste, if you don't like me...acquire some taste.

The time it takes for you to fall out with fake friends, you can be two house and $250,000 up.

You let your kids out of your sight, they are going to sight see.

Happiness is an inside job.

You Pops got that old school game, call me Atari.

I work airport hours, Sunday to Sunday.

When you're air dry fresh, you don't need a hanger.

Just stop where you began.... mistakes.

Honeycomb For Young Cubs, Vol. 1

I look good. I smell good. I feel good.

Once you get the picture you can get up out the frame.

A wise man can see royalty in a peasant. Royalty sees a peasant in a wise man. A peasant thinks he sees wisdom in royalty.

The warrior only sees victory or defeat. The religious only sees heaven or hell.

Stop at nothing if you are after something.

Truth is a matter of consequences.

To lie is a tough way to live but an effortless way to die slow.

There is no path to happiness. Happiness is the path.

Say less, listen more.

Tighten my belt before you ask for help.

All this, and Heaven too?

We get approx. 27,000 days to live. Live them all to the fullest.

Sometimes the juice just ain't worth the squeeze.

There is a difference between pace and stride.

People with a big head, usually it's all hat.

It is the fate of glass to break.

Maintenance does not stimulate production.

The best way to protect your kid is to disappoint them.

What you do not know is bigger than you.

Death is the enemy, from the first to the last.

Character is like a tree and reputation like its shadow.

Life is like baseball. Relationships are like football. Friendship is like basketball.

Honeycomb For Young Cubs, Vol. 1

It's hard to be hungry when you're full.

Be born in not sworn in.

Dream big. Do big.

My diamonds be mingling, not singling.

You won't catch fish watching someone else's line.

Get rich or ride bitch.

Keep your mind on cash, and your grind on smash.

Stay tombstone ready, take shit off nobody.

Make your dream better by making your scheme better.

Everybody wants to be fly, but don't want to be maggot first.

I exaggerate the example to drive home my point.

Life isn't fair.... a fair is where you go for silly prizes and clowns.

To defend everything, is to be credible on nothing.

Division and prison come from a lack of vision.

Mistakes are the portal to discovery.

Truth can be a matter of circumstance to the uninitiated.

The strong gets tested and the weak gets rested.

In all your getting, get some understanding.

After a setback, the goal is to go from fell off to well off.

Deflects praise and accept criticism.

Live a good life and grow old.

Never commit the sin of turning your back on time.

Honeycomb For Young Cubs, Vol. 1

Keep your swag on coffin and your bag on overflow.

Ask no question, get no lies.

If you look like money, then you just might make some.

Recover from the fumble, do not take a knee.

First you crawl, then you fall, it's the only way to ball.

You get no credit or commendation for doing what you're supposed to do.

When it comes to credit, always be slow to take and quick to give.

Institution, prostitution, evolution, or revolution. Choose one.

Financial freedom is legacy.

The sparkle depends on the flaws in the diamond.

We don't get burnt out by what we do, we get burnt out when we forget why we're doing it.

Presence is much more impactful than provision.

As a man, we just need someone to love that unconditionally loves us back. If you can't give us that, then give us something to hope for. And if you can't give us that, then give me something to do.

This life, it's too early to give up and too late to do anything else.

It's okay to bring sand to the beach if your beach is better.

Didn't grow up with it, so I had to go get it.

I don't want to hear about what you heard. I would rather hear about what you read.

I don't make any big decisions too long after sunset or too far from sunrise.

We are all nothing more than what we choose to reveal.

There is no better way to overpower a trickle of doubt than an over flood of naked truth.

Honeycomb For Young Cubs, Vol. 1

I love you like sharks love blood in the water.

In corporate America where everyone is so busy reinventing themselves, be your best authentic self.

When you're prepared, you're never scared.

Don't rock the boat while we're sitting in it because it will be hard to save both of us.

Being chill don't pay the bills.

Live for today, plan for tomorrow, hustle like you about to lose it all.

Anticipate a man's actions based on his character, judge him by his principles.

Inspect what you expect.

At the casino, when the dealer says: Good luck = fuck you; thank you, sir = dummy.

If you think you can live in this world and not be part of it, then that is a mistake.

Set expectations so there is clear understanding of goals.

Actions produce consequences.

Men who seek redemption are always in a place far removed from reality.

Any belief that forgiveness from sin is painless is a child's thought.

You can't buy anything with grief. Grief is worthless.

You live the world that you create, therefore you live in the world you have made.

Nothing is as cruel in life than a coward, and there is nothing more elegant than a hunter.

The good news is that we know why we fail. The bad news is that we also know it's at our own doing.

Sometimes you win, sometimes you learn.

Establish a situation where the people and product collisions are unique to your business only.

Honeycomb For Young Cubs, Vol. 1

Love and pain can't be experienced one without the other.

Get money, stay true.

Read - The Wealth Choice, by Dennis Kimbrough.

In life, if you never took a chance then you never had a chance.

Getting it right is more important than being right.

You can never change the people around you, so change the people around you.

Lions never play with monkeys.

As long as there is will, there is a way.

Never turn a wolf into a house pet.

What got you here won't get you there.

The grass is always greener where you water it.

When you live the life you love, you love the life that you live.

People always want your honest opinion, until you give them one.

The first thing to learn about being a winner, is learning how not to lose.

Whether you think you can or think you can't…you're right.

For a straight line to make sense, one would have had to first seen a crooked line.

If you put a King in a circus, it doesn't look like a palace. Rather, the King looks like a clown.

In friendships, you want volunteers not hostages.

Comparison is the thief to joy.

Once is an accident. Twice is a trend. Three times is a problem.

When you're up, that's when everybody is down for you.

Honeycomb For Young Cubs, Vol. 1

Never let a hard time humble you.

Using nostalgia for empathy only works when you're selling something.

There is no love without losing, and no life without bruising.

We all have vices. The problems come when we abuse them.

90% of life is showing up. The other 10% is hard work.

The function of man is to exist.

When greatness calls, be ready.

Mortality beats a heavy drum.

Altitude is required for eagles. Gratitude is mandatory for pigeons.

Fear is not a door, it's a mirror.

You can be whatever you visualize.

Don't raise your voice, improve your argument.

Habits and choices form your identity.

If wishes were horses, then beggars would ride.

The remedy is in the poison.

Never live for praise because you will die by criticism.

God does not call the qualified. God qualifies the called.

Romance is a costly pleasure.

When you come up, some people feelings come out.

Whenever something good is trying to happen something bad is trying to stop it.

Sometimes, the surgery is a success, but the patient dies.

Achieve escape velocity and move away from where you were born. See the world.

Honeycomb For Young Cubs, Vol. 1

Trust is more valuable than love.

Grace, you earn. Forgiveness, you seek. Closure, you find.

I hear and I forget. I see and I remember. I do and I understand.

For God gave us a spirit not of fear, but of power, love and self-control. 2 Timothy 1:7

Honeycomb For Young Cubs, Vol. 1

Omega.

Tom, Jewel, Rosalind, and Bonnie Sherman – thank you.

Made in the USA
Columbia, SC
22 June 2025

Honeycomb For Young Cubs, Vol. 1

Anybody willing to put in hard work will always have dirt under their fingernails.

You have to give all of yourself to something if you are ever to reach greatness.

Skill requires repetition.

If you dominate for a year, it's your season. If you dominate a few years, it's your era. If you dominate a few decades, it's your dynasty.

If you have $10, spend only $3 and save $7. This is how you achieve wealth and stay prepared for a rainy day.

Change and blessings come only with time.

Correlation does not equate to causality.

Two wrongs do not make a right. Two Wrights did make an airplane.

Having a plan and doing it are two different things.

Be the best you. Be yourself. Don't ever try to be like another man.

Find happiness in all your choices, all that you do. There will certainly be obstacles and setbacks, however this is part of life. What matters is how you accept and overcome them. This is what measures your character.

When it comes to your individual mental peace and stability, refuse to be anything but okay. Guard your peace.

When in a relationship, you will learn ugly lessons from a pretty woman/handsome man.

A person's politics is just like their religion: it doesn't require you to believe the same, nor does it require your opinion.

Freedom is an illusion. No man's actions are free from consequence.

Have you ever seen a chrome crown?

Removed listening is insulting, people feel that you're not engaged or involved. Reactive listening is infuriating, you're taking everything personally. Responsible listening is listening as usual. Receptive listening is empathic; it tries to genuinely understand and respond to the other person.

Honeycomb For Young Cubs, Vol. 1

Unprecedented doesn't have to mean defeated. Allow the unknown to be opportunity for innovation.

Love + Honor + Loyalty = Family.

Opportunity is on the other side of chaos.

Everybody's mad at you when you are living fabulous, self-made mean never out here kissing asses.

New levels bring new devils.

Money is like water. If you pitch your tent, make sure it's near a source that can easily be accessed and can be replenished. Make sure it's a clean source, not dirty. Don't walk around this world looking and being thirsty - not a good way to be, not a good look. Make sure you're not caught in a drought and unable to sustain yourself. You can die of dehydration, so keep plenty of 'water' nearby.

The price of greatness is responsibility. Responsibility is an investment.

You can't make the same mistake twice, the second time it's no longer a mistake, it's a choice.

Knowing who you are is hard. Eliminating who you are not even harder.

In this world, a man just wants to be treated like a king in his own home. At home, we just want our partner to love us without condition. Nothing more.

I'm so ahead of my time, I'm about to start another life.

Respect is not earned twice, once you lose it then it's gone.

Better to be seen than viewed.

Grind all winter, shine all summer.

Paranoid of poverty.

My drive...25/8 no brakes.

Resistance to tyranny is obedience to God.

Nine out of ten worries are usually unfounded and self-imposed.

Honeycomb For Young Cubs, Vol. 1

We work with what we have, not what we wish for.

Getting out of something is always tougher than getting in.

Paradise lost is paradise gained.

People don't know your whole story; they just know the chapter they met you on.

Many are called yest few are chosen.

Rise and grind. Wake up and cake up. Don't sleep your life away.

Do the best with what God gives you.

When you're fighting with yourself, against those demons and monkeys on your back, and you're losing that fight.... what comes next is you fighting those closest to you. Taking an unnecessary fight to them that they did not deserve. Don't do that.

Never plan for a setback. Always plan for a comeback.

Put your tongue in park. Never run your mouth.

Do not be a fake like a fire drill.

A smooth sea never made a skilled sailor.

Isn't it fun to try to do the impossible?

You like someone for their qualities but love them for their defects.

If they did not invite you, don't ever ask to go.

What makes a man a man? Is it his origins? His views on life? I don't think so. It's the choices he makes. Not how he starts things, but how he decides to end them.

Wisdom is peace. Ignorance is chaos.

You will never win at life if you lose your mind.

Because you are alive, everything is possible.

Time is wealth, share it generously with family and friends.

Act your wage.

Honeycomb For Young Cubs, Vol. 1

Don't hate on anybody and don't wait on anybody.

If something is to be empty, let it be your stomach but never your pockets.

What you would do eventually, you should do immediately.

Trouble never sends a warning.

Life is what your soul costs. Make life worth it.

Don't strive to make news, strive to be the main topic.

Admiration can easily turn into hatred, which then also turn into suicide of self.

Have a funeral for all your bad habits.

I don't trust a man that puts his back against the wall. I trust a man that puts his back against the cross.

We're all links in a chain.

FEAR - false evidence appearing real.

Where you stand is where you sit.

When it comes to family, we can either hang together or hang separately.

If you don't talk about it, you're not working on it.

Rise and grind.

You can't break a stick that's part of a bundle.

Belief isn't what you say, it's what you do.

When you're a lion, you have to walk slow and growl low when around sheep.

If people are tired of how you live, they will die exhausted.

Stop at nothing if you're after something.

Subtract everything out of your life that's not adding up.

Honeycomb For Young Cubs, Vol. 1

Make shit shake until it break.

Every day is a payday, no days off.

When you make cake and get bread, you accumulate calories.

The future is now.

Living ain't for everybody, most people are waiting to die.

Avoid trick knowledge.

Love is the highest elevation of understanding.

Time is the currency of progress.

Straighten up or get your ass tore up.

Success is not a straight line.

There is no heaven without dying.

Toast - May we always get what we want, but never what we deserve.

Toast - Good bread, good meat. Good God let's eat.

Make your mess your message.

Good seeds make good trees.

Never mix your feelings with your dealings.

Being blind is having sight but no vision.

What can't be cured must be endured.

In life, there are no instant rebates.

Do not ever let anyone get the best of you, even if they want the best for you.

You can always make something out of what you've been made out to be.

We accept the love that we think we deserve.

Honeycomb For Young Cubs, Vol. 1

In life, no one wins...one side just loses slowly.

I have two words for you: two words.

Sometimes when you elevate, friends separate.

Man's reach exceeds his grasp. Man's grasp exceeds his nerve. Man's nerve exceeds his imagination.

Reach beyond your own bubble.

Come from ordinary beginnings, then achieve extraordinary accomplishments.

Existential dilemmas....do or don't. Will or won't.

Drink the stress, gargle the pain, and spit bullshit out of your system.

Save until it hurts.

Pigs get fat, hogs get slaughtered.

Give way.

Be where your feet are.

Hope not, hope gets the poorly prepared killed.

I'm an acquired taste, if you don't like me...acquire some taste.

The time it takes for you to fall out with fake friends, you can be two house and $250,000 up.

You let your kids out of your sight, they are going to sight see.

Happiness is an inside job.

You Pops got that old school game, call me Atari.

I work airport hours, Sunday to Sunday.

When you're air dry fresh, you don't need a hanger.

Just stop where you began.... mistakes.

Honeycomb For Young Cubs, Vol. 1

I look good. I smell good. I feel good.

Once you get the picture you can get up out the frame.

A wise man can see royalty in a peasant. Royalty sees a peasant in a wise man. A peasant thinks he sees wisdom in royalty.

The warrior only sees victory or defeat. The religious only sees heaven or hell.

Stop at nothing if you are after something.

Truth is a matter of consequences.

To lie is a tough way to live but an effortless way to die slow.

There is no path to happiness. Happiness is the path.

Say less, listen more.

Tighten my belt before you ask for help.

All this, and Heaven too?

We get approx. 27,000 days to live. Live them all to the fullest.

Sometimes the juice just ain't worth the squeeze.

There is a difference between pace and stride.

People with a big head, usually it's all hat.

It is the fate of glass to break.

Maintenance does not stimulate production.

The best way to protect your kid is to disappoint them.

What you do not know is bigger than you.

Death is the enemy, from the first to the last.

Character is like a tree and reputation like its shadow.

Life is like baseball. Relationships are like football. Friendship is like basketball.

Honeycomb For Young Cubs, Vol. 1

It's hard to be hungry when you're full.

Be born in not sworn in.

Dream big. Do big.

My diamonds be mingling, not singling.

You won't catch fish watching someone else's line.

Get rich or ride bitch.

Keep your mind on cash, and your grind on smash.

Stay tombstone ready, take shit off nobody.

Make your dream better by making your scheme better.

Everybody wants to be fly, but don't want to be maggot first.

I exaggerate the example to drive home my point.

Life isn't fair.... a fair is where you go for silly prizes and clowns.

To defend everything, is to be credible on nothing.

Division and prison come from a lack of vision.

Mistakes are the portal to discovery.

Truth can be a matter of circumstance to the uninitiated.

The strong gets tested and the weak gets rested.

In all your getting, get some understanding.

After a setback, the goal is to go from fell off to well off.

Deflects praise and accept criticism.

Live a good life and grow old.

Never commit the sin of turning your back on time.

Honeycomb For Young Cubs, Vol. 1

Keep your swag on coffin and your bag on overflow.

Ask no question, get no lies.

If you look like money, then you just might make some.

Recover from the fumble, do not take a knee.

First you crawl, then you fall, it's the only way to ball.

You get no credit or commendation for doing what you're supposed to do.

When it comes to credit, always be slow to take and quick to give.

Institution, prostitution, evolution, or revolution. Choose one.

Financial freedom is legacy.

The sparkle depends on the flaws in the diamond.

We don't get burnt out by what we do, we get burnt out when we forget why we're doing it.

Presence is much more impactful than provision.

As a man, we just need someone to love that unconditionally loves us back. If you can't give us that, then give us something to hope for. And if you can't give us that, then give me something to do.

This life, it's too early to give up and too late to do anything else.

It's okay to bring sand to the beach if your beach is better.

Didn't grow up with it, so I had to go get it.

I don't want to hear about what you heard. I would rather hear about what you read.

I don't make any big decisions too long after sunset or too far from sunrise.

We are all nothing more than what we choose to reveal.

There is no better way to overpower a trickle of doubt than an over flood of naked truth.

Honeycomb For Young Cubs, Vol. 1

I love you like sharks love blood in the water.

In corporate America where everyone is so busy reinventing themselves, be your best authentic self.

When you're prepared, you're never scared.

Don't rock the boat while we're sitting in it because it will be hard to save both of us.

Being chill don't pay the bills.

Live for today, plan for tomorrow, hustle like you about to lose it all.

Anticipate a man's actions based on his character, judge him by his principles.

Inspect what you expect.

At the casino, when the dealer says: Good luck = fuck you; thank you, sir = dummy.

If you think you can live in this world and not be part of it, then that is a mistake.

Set expectations so there is clear understanding of goals.

Actions produce consequences.

Men who seek redemption are always in a place far removed from reality.

Any belief that forgiveness from sin is painless is a child's thought.

You can't buy anything with grief. Grief is worthless.

You live the world that you create, therefore you live in the world you have made.

Nothing is as cruel in life than a coward, and there is nothing more elegant than a hunter.

The good news is that we know why we fail. The bad news is that we also know it's at our own doing.

Sometimes you win, sometimes you learn.

Establish a situation where the people and product collisions are unique to your business only.

Honeycomb For Young Cubs, Vol. 1

Love and pain can't be experienced one without the other.

Get money, stay true.

Read - The Wealth Choice, by Dennis Kimbrough.

In life, if you never took a chance then you never had a chance.

Getting it right is more important than being right.

You can never change the people around you, so change the people around you.

Lions never play with monkeys.

As long as there is will, there is a way.

Never turn a wolf into a house pet.

What got you here won't get you there.

The grass is always greener where you water it.

When you live the life you love, you love the life that you live.

People always want your honest opinion, until you give them one.

The first thing to learn about being a winner, is learning how not to lose.

Whether you think you can or think you can't...you're right.

For a straight line to make sense, one would have had to first seen a crooked line.

If you put a King in a circus, it doesn't look like a palace. Rather, the King looks like a clown.

In friendships, you want volunteers not hostages.

Comparison is the thief to joy.

Once is an accident. Twice is a trend. Three times is a problem.

When you're up, that's when everybody is down for you.

Honeycomb For Young Cubs, Vol. 1

Never let a hard time humble you.

Using nostalgia for empathy only works when you're selling something.

There is no love without losing, and no life without bruising.

We all have vices. The problems come when we abuse them.

90% of life is showing up. The other 10% is hard work.

The function of man is to exist.

When greatness calls, be ready.

Mortality beats a heavy drum.

Altitude is required for eagles. Gratitude is mandatory for pigeons.

Fear is not a door, it's a mirror.

You can be whatever you visualize.

Don't raise your voice, improve your argument.

Habits and choices form your identity.

If wishes were horses, then beggars would ride.

The remedy is in the poison.

Never live for praise because you will die by criticism.

God does not call the qualified. God qualifies the called.

Romance is a costly pleasure.

When you come up, some people feelings come out.

Whenever something good is trying to happen something bad is trying to stop it.

Sometimes, the surgery is a success, but the patient dies.

Achieve escape velocity and move away from where you were born. See the world.

Trust is more valuable than love.

Grace, you earn. Forgiveness, you seek. Closure, you find.

I hear and I forget. I see and I remember. I do and I understand.

For God gave us a spirit not of fear, but of power, love and self-control. 2 Timothy 1:7

Honeycomb For Young Cubs, Vol. 1

Omega.

Tom, Jewel, Rosalind, and Bonnie Sherman – thank you.

Made in the USA
Columbia, SC
22 June 2025